Global Utopian Kingdom

By: Iman-Utopia Layjou Bah

INTRODUCTION

Brothers and Sisters, there is nothing more beautiful in principle than the ideal of a global utopian kingdom, nor is there anything more beautiful in form. There is no goal more worthy, nor any promise truer. I, even I, wholeheartedly believe that the establishment of a global utopian kingdom will be mankind's greatest triumph, that it is the highest ideal we can collectively aspire to, and as so, should be the guiding star of all our collective efforts. A utopia is a community in which conditions are optimal for individuals to pursue happiness, one in which all enjoy Liberty, Justice, Peace, and Prosperity. Creating such conditions is the best we can collectively do for one another, and by doing so, we will have perfected our duty to one another. So, We shall proceed to outline the steps we can take to bring forth the kingdom, briefly describe life within it, and offer key truths and insights pertinent to attaining and maintaining the kingdom.

PART I:
THE STEPS TOWARDS ESTABLISHING THE KINGDOM

OPENING REMARKS ON THE STEPS TOWARDS ESTABLISHING THE KINGDOM

Straight not will be the path towards establishing a global utopian kingdom. The following illustration of the steps to be taken on this path and the order thereof is to serve only as a guidance, a guidance given authority by the urgency of moral duty and influenced by consideration of practical and logistical feasibility. As we the people embark on this journey, difficulties, challenges, and obstacles, both foreseen and unforeseen, will surely present themselves, and changes in strategy and approach may be of order. So and so, in thus manner, with these seven steps, can the kingdom be brought into being:

STEP 1: END HUNGER

Robbing of life and inflicting constant suffering on its victims, hunger is by far the most urgent of challenges to be overcome. The nourishment produced by Mother Earth indeed suffices to sustain and energize all of her children, and all must be allowed to partake of her bounty. Industry and labor is to be organized so to make fertile lands fruitful, farms shall be increased in number, as shall food processing factories. Civil leaders shall identify communities most in need, logistical experts shall map out and oversee the distribution of food. Communities shall take care that no member of their own community succumbs to hunger, individuals shall take care that food waste is minimized. As hunger is reduced, so shall be reduced misery, suffering, and despair. As misery, suffering, and despair are reduced, so shall be reduced animosity, instability, and fear. As the strength of the malnourished grows, so shall optimism and moral fortitude. As optimism and moral fortitude grow, so shall the collective capacity to secure peace and prosperity.

STEP 2: END EXTREME THIRST

As victory over hunger draws near, clean water must begin to flow to the thirsty, and so too, to they who must settle for impure water. Extreme thirst is agonizing and defeating, and the drinking of impure water risky and compromising.. urgently, does duty demand the provision of clean water. States and labor shall be mobilized so to redirect clean water from areas in which it is abundant to areas in need. Also shall desalination plants be constructed, wells and channels dug, rainwater basins deployed, lakes and rivers tapped. As water flows to the thirsty, the mighty tides of desperation and hopelessness shall subside, and lo! Ships sailing to the Promised Land will be more secure.

STEP 3: CLOTHE ALL

As thirst is being quenched, clothing must begin to make its way to the naked and otherwise exposed. This most basic of needs is the first line of defense against insects, sun rays, and the elements, and none shall be denied this necessity. Unused clothing shall be donated and directed where needed, and if necessary, cotton shall be farmed, and other fabrics produced at higher volumes. Suitable dress increases one's dignity, and as one is being lifted by an increase in dignity, an increase in strength of character may follow. When there is an abundance of strength of character in a land, the people therein inevitably prosper.

STEP 4: SHELTER ALL

Much strength of character will be necessary to complete for all the provision of basic needs. Much mental and physical toil too, shall be required as we act to provide shelter for all. Yet alas, we must do so, for no one contributing to society, or willing to do so when called upon, need suffer the indignity and injury of not having a place to call home, of lacking adequate protection from Mother Nature and the elements, of not having a place to entertain family and friends, of not having a place to retreat to privacy and enjoy serenity. Thus can also be said for those who are unable to contribute to society due to illnesses of the mind or body, or limitations thereof. As for they who are of sound mind and body yet desire not to contribute to society out of sloth, rebelliousness, or contempt, the people are morally obliged not to provide for them shelter, though if the people do so out of mercy and generosity, such shall be very well and very good. For those whom society is morally obliged to shelter, the state shall assist in acquiring land. Industry shall be mobilized to procure building material, and labor contracted to construct or add to developed living communities. As the unsheltered become housed and the basic needs of every man, woman, and child are completely provided for, the urgency of moral duty shall be tempered and clarity of mind will be more readily had. Verily, tranquility will then descend upon peoples everywhere.. When hunger and thirst hamstrung none and all have a place to call home, exalted shall be the state of mankind, and the loftiest of goals, The Global Utopian Kingdom, shall be in reach.

STEP 5: ESTABLISH THE CONDITIONS FOR PERPETUAL PEACE

As none no longer suffer from lack of any basic need and the people bask in tranquility and clarity of mind, work must begin on establishing the conditions for perpetual peace. The people shall unequivocally and emphatically declare war an unacceptable means of resolving disputes. So too, shall the people declare any instigator of war (or any form of organized violence) an enemy of all, and subject to severe punishment. Once the people have declared thus, nations shall proceed to do away with all capacity to wage war and to destroy all instruments of war. The elimination of nuclear weapons and the means to develop such shall take precedence. The destruction of bombs and missiles shall follow, then the decommissioning of warplanes and warships. The disbanding of all national armies shall complete this process and bring lasting peace nearer to all. Indeed, the dissipation of the clouds of war will increase in luminescence the lights illuminating the path towards a brighter future for all, and the silencing of the drums of war will make the rhythms of life more harmonious.

STEP 6: ESTABLISH THE KINGDOM

As nations lay aside their arms for the sake of peace and harmony, so too shall they lay aside their national interests and proceed to unite and form a single government, a global kingdom, thereby reducing division, competition, and cause for conflict among peoples. The mandate of this government shall be to serve as the supreme guarantor of justice and liberty and to promote peace and prosperity. It shall be a meritocracy, and he who is deemed the wisest, justest, and most capable of the people shall be appointed King and preside over this government. The king shall exercise no direct power over the people, but shall serve the people as the chief executive of the government and Supreme Arbiter. Individual cities and towns shall serve as the base and loci of power, and no division of the government is to assume any power, duty, or responsibility better left to the people. A unity of state shall promote unity among all peoples, so too shall it strengthen the connections and bonds between them. A more united people is a stronger and more efficacious people, and will meet with more success in pursuing common goals, and in the individual pursuits of happiness.

STEP 7: UTOPIANIZE THE KINGDOM

As unity takes root and the kingdom forms, work shall begin on creating utopian conditions in all communities, that is, on optimizing the conditions in which individuals pursue happiness. The nature of this work will vary with the geographic location of different communities and the particular characteristics and values of the people therein, and so too, may the nature of this work change as times change, and eras begin and end. Even so, some work shall be common to all communities, such as the work of providing and maintaining a healthy living environment for all. The work of establishing and maintaining utopian conditions shall be the business of life within the kingdom and be forever ongoing. It shall be carried out by the people, with The State playing a supplementary role where necessary. Once utopian conditions have been established in every community, humanity will have alas realized a global utopian kingdom. And lo! On that day, the sun shall be more radiant than ever, nightfall more peaceful than ever. The smiles of men and women shall be brighter, their eyes stiller. The life force coursing through the universe shall be more electric than ever, the planet more lively than ever. Society will have ascended from a state of becoming, into that of being..

CLOSING REMARKS ON THE STEPS TOWARDS ESTABLISHING THE KINGDOM

In such manner, with these seven steps, can the global utopian kingdom be brought into being. The completion of this journey will require much moral fortitude, determination, toil, and patience. So too, will it require individuals to view and think about the world differently, and a global paradigm shift. Yea, this illustration has been much oversimplified, yet certain is its promise. The details this illustration is want for will undoubtedly manifest themselves by way of the brilliance and ingenuity of the people when circumstances necessitate them. Yet alas, we the people must will to rise and stand before the first step can be taken..

PART II: LIFE WITHIN THE KINGDOM

CHAPTER 1: THE CONDITIONS OF LIFE

The conditions of life within the kingdom are to be optimal for the individual pursuit of happiness. Now, individual communities shall ultimately determine what specific conditions amount to being optimal, though still, certain conditions shall indeed be common to all, such as an environment conducive to good health. In such an environment, healthy food is available, the water is clean, the air safe to breathe, fitness and recreation centers are accessible, as are hospitals and other healthcare resources. Another common condition of life shall be that the contributing members of every community, along with the immature, the elderly, and those prevented from work due to physical or mental limitations, shall enjoy a home equipped with electricity and indoor plumbing. And also, every individual throughout the kingdom shall be privy to the unequivocal and unqualified support and defense of his or her right to liberty and justice, that is, the right to engage in whatever activities one may, to venture wherever one may, and to be afforded recourse and redress upon suffering an unjust infringement of his or her rights. If this guarantee is not upheld by one's community, then it will be done so by The State.

CHAPTER 2: THE ROLE & NATURE OF THE STATE

In the kingdom, to the greatest extent possible, every individual is to be the governor of his or her affairs, every family the governor of its affairs. The role of the state shall be to carry out its mandate of serving as the supreme guarantor of liberty and justice for all persons and of promoting peace and prosperity, as well as to do that which is difficult for the people to do themselves. Every city and town, though only one of numerous divisions comprising the united and all-encompassing worldwide government, shall also be the governor of its own affairs, and be fully responsible for providing its citizens full access to the services of the state, though it may seek and be granted additional assistance from higher divisions of the state when necessary. The state shall be large enough to carry out its mandate and maintain the public peace, yet too small to expand its powers beyond this mandate or quell a general insurrection, so that the people may always overpower the state and never be overpowered by the state. The role of the state shall not be to function as ruler over the people, but to be a supporter of the people in their pursuit of happiness. Also, the state, through the king and his viceroys, shall serve as an impartial arbiter in unresolvable disputes between peoples and businesses, so that conflict can be averted, and peace and harmony maintained.

CHAPTER 3: TRADE, COMMERCE, ECONOMICS, & WORK

Throughout the kingdom, trade and commerce shall be governed by free market principles and all who are able will be expected to work and contribute to the economy and welfare of The Kingdom, though those who are occupied with the raising of children or with tending to the needs of loved ones who are elderly, ill, or incapacitated, may be excused from such obligations. Businesses shall be free to operate in any community that welcomes them, individuals free to buy and sell what they will. No unwarranted interference in the economy by the state shall be permitted. Any laws or regulations issued by The State governing trade and commerce shall without exception be in accord with its mandate of guaranteeing liberty and justice and promoting peace and prosperity. In accord with this mandate, the state may see to it that resources are utilized at a sustainable pace, and that goods and services are so distributed that the needs of all are met. And to the greatest extent possible, individuals shall be given the opportunity to work and contribute to society in a way they themselves deem most suitable to their nature and talents, and the economy shall be so managed that none will be under the necessity of dedicating more than one-third of their waking hours to work. Thereby, all may have ample time to fulfill the various non work related obligations of life and pursue happiness.

PART III:
KEY TRUTHS &
INSIGHTS

1.   The world is what it is today, and will be what it will be tomorrow because the masses have desired it so, or accepted that it is so; we the people can shape the world in whichever way we deem fit.

2.   The overarching task of life is the work of coexisting with one another and other life forms in a harmonious manner, and this simple truth must be kept in mind lest we cause ourselves unnecessary confusion and difficulty.

3.   Coexisting harmoniously with other people is neither simple nor easy, and it is among the great challenges of life. However, when those coexisting among one another live virtuously and behave ethically towards each other, much difficulty is removed from the task.

4.   Maintaining peaceful and harmonious relations often requires sacrifice, as does the accomplishing of great feats. Sacrifices on a scale perhaps never seen before will be required if mankind is to establish and maintain peace and harmony throughout the earth.

5.   The very nature of human beings, with our differences in personality and interests, and with our flaws and shortcomings, guarantees that disagreements and conflicts will inevitably arise as we endeavor to coexist with one another peacefully, and therefore perpetual and undisturbed harmony is unrealistic. However, if violence and warfare are not resorted to, the public peace may be maintained.

6.   There almost certainly will always be individuals who do not embrace society, and who are mischievous, rebellious, and who seek to cause trouble; this is part of the challenge of life and should not be cause for pessimism.

7.   The widespread practice of virtue alone will resolve many of mankind's problems; immoral conduct and the practice of vice is the greatest threat to social stability and the individual pursuits of happiness.

8.   It is imperative that society is so organized that it is as easy as possible for individuals to practice virtue, for part of being human is having weaknesses and vices, and these are more difficult to overcome when encouraged or supported by social structure.

9.   Life can be seen as an endless series of choices, often of such nature: practice virtue or practice vice? Be selfish or be selfless?? If The Kingdom is to be brought into being, the masses must muster the strength to practice virtue and be selfless, over and over and over again..

10. Prioritization is necessary whenever there are multiple issues in need of being addressed; the provision of the basic needs of all human beings (food, water, clothing, and housing) must take precedence over all other issues facing humanity.

11. The earth is endowed with resources such that it can adequately support all life herein; none need go without.

12. If greed is held in check, not only will all enjoy sufficiency, but it may very well be possible that all will enjoy abundance.

13. To the extent that all human beings are seen as part of one big family, and to the extent that the entire earth and all its resources is seen as the common inheritance of all, is the extent that mankind will know peace and prosperity.

14. One's character is diminished by the refusal to make small sacrifices that can prevent another from enduring significant suffering. This is why although some individuals are undeserving of food in that they refuse to work and contribute to society, it still is important that society nonetheless allow such a one to access food, at least the bare minimum to survive and prolong life -and possibly transform into a willing contributor to society.

15. The misuse and overuse of natural resources harms the conditions of life, so individuals, as well as society as a whole, have a moral duty to utilize resources in a modest and sustainable fashion.

16. The natural beauty of the earth and that of what exists therein is dear to a great many of people, and as so, reasonable efforts must be made to preserve it.

17. Injustice is an enemy of all and must be combatted wherever it arises -without exception.

18. No expense should be spared in the effort to guarantee justice to all and to do so expediently, whether that means funding the salaries of judges and lawyers, building courthouses and tribunals, or the doing of whatever else that may be necessary.

19. The fate of criminals and the rendering of judgements and punishments is best left in the hands of experts of moral philosophy and those of proven character, so that none may be subject to unnecessarily cruel and harsh punishments.

20. All human beings are invaluable, however, individuals are not equal in talent, ability, strength, or determination, so naturally some achieve more success and gain more wealth than others. Equality is a noble goal, but it is imperative that society not unjustly limit or take from the gains of the gifted.

21. Human labor, natural resources, and knowledge has real value, currency does not; it is just a convenient medium of exchange. The people must never feel powerless for lack of money, and the lack thereof should never prevent the doing of good.

22. Natural disparities in wealth should be expected and tolerated for in any socioeconomic system, some individuals by their inherent nature will become wealthier than others. However, when a class of individuals becomes extremely wealthy while another becomes extremely impoverished, such is problematic and should not be tolerated.

23. Better is always good, and at times it is necessary to temporarily settle for better until that which is ideal can be had. For example, it would be ideal for every family to have a sizable and comfortable home, yet, some who were previously homeless may have to be placed in hotel like structures until an ideal home can be had.

24. There is inherent dignity in every human life, and by simply recognizing and respecting this, the causes of Liberty, Justice, Peace, and Prosperity can all be furthered.

25. Loyalty to humanity as a whole and commitment to ethical standards must take precedence over loyalty and commitment to theories and dogmas, ideologies, political parties, and special interests.

26. For people to be able to choose their own leaders (Democracy) is good, but better still is when those occupying leadership positions are the most capable of performing the duties of their office. Meritocracy is the best form of government, and such a government will be most effective in serving the needs of the people.

27. Good, wise, and just leadership shall take humanity to heights never reached before in the modern era. Such leadership is invaluable and indispensable, and the recruitment of such leadership must be carried out with the utmost seriousness and earnestness.

28. The leaders of a state need be the wisest, justest, and most capable administrators from among the people and should maintain independence from the people so that they are not led by the capriciousness of the people to make poor decisions, though it is still necessary that the people at all times retain the power to remove leaders when there is sufficient grounds and support to do so.

29. The mere existence and presence of both weapons of war and standing armies is a threat to peace in general as well as to peace of mind; both must be done away with.

30. It can be expected that countries will be hesitant if not completely unwilling to disarm and destroy all capacity to wage war, therefore it is necessary that the people love peace enough to vehemently demand and oversee the doing of such.

31. No governmental institution, company, or organization truly has power; all power ultimately lies with the people, and we the people must always feel empowered.

32. Disruption of the status quo at times results in fierce resistance, particularly from those who benefit from it, and establishing a global utopian kingdom would amount to utterly upending the global status quo; much fighting should be expected in order to bring The Kingdom into being.

33. To unite all governments into one global state will be a logistical and administrative feat the likes of which the world has never seen, but the doing of such will produce a unity the likes of which has never been felt, and produce wholesome fruit the likes of which has never been tasted.

34. Unity is hard to achieve, and even harder to maintain. Atrophy, a symptom of time, erodes the strength of commitments and undercurrents of animosity undermine loyalty. The men and women of a union must be strong as well as vigilant in exercising strength to uphold it.

35. Those who govern should be as close as possible to the governed so that they may be as responsive and as sympathetic as possible to the needs of the people; it is better that a city exercise power over a people than that a provincial government do so, better that a provincial government do so than a regional government, a regional government than a global government.

36. Every type of person that is needed by society exists, from the ingenious and inventive, to the wise and virtuous, to the strong and brave, to the caring and nurturing, to the creative and artistic, so on and so forth. If individuals are granted the space and opportunity to develop into the best version of themselves, they will find their own way of contributing to society and advancing the cause of humanity.

37. As long as an individual is not committing an injustice, he or she must be given the space and opportunity to be exactly who they want to be and to do exactly as they please; the state and society at large must not contrive to change a person or interfere in his or her affairs, though loved ones and concerned members of his community can rightly guide, caution, and counsel him.

38. The purpose of any educational system for the development of the youth should be to best prepare them to contribute to society and lead a happy, fulfilling life. And in order to accomplish this, an educational system must focus heavily on cultivating virtue, morality, and character.

39. No expense should be spared in order to adequately raise and educate the youth, for an intelligent, respectful, and well-rounded young adult is an invaluable asset to society.

40. There is no shortage of brilliant individuals and ideas in this world, and to know such individuals and ideas, is to be certain that solutions can be found to the various problems humanity faces.

41. There is no shortage of good people willing to do good works in order to further the cause of humanity, and moreover, there are countless people who currently populate the earth who need no convincing in order to be willing to contribute to a worthy cause.

42. The wise application of science and technology in bettering the conditions of life will greatly reduce the difficulty in establishing utopian conditions throughout the earth.

43. If individuals are to reach their full potential, and thus humanity as a whole, society, with particular focus on the economy, must be reorganized such that individuals, if they so will, enjoy ample time to cultivate virtue and realize personal growth, continue to learn, tend to the needs of family members, be charitable, give and receive love, exercise, enjoy rest and recreation, and explore the world and have adventures.

44. Even under ideal conditions, some will struggle to find happiness and fulfillment. Most fortunately, there exists a type of person who enjoys helping others find happiness, and is perfectly willing to do so.

45. Suffering is a fact of life, and even when a global utopian kingdom is established and humanity reaches its full potential, life will never be all good for all people all the time. However, if unity and strength of character abound, most people will enjoy a happy existence most of the time, and this is the best that can be done.

CONCLUSION

And so Brothers and Sisters, we must have a collective vision and purpose, and there is no vision more beautiful than that of the global utopian kingdom, nor any purpose more worthy. Let us not waste time and energy on vain and shallow pursuits nor waste life and treasure maintaining a world that is unbecoming of dignified and virtuous human beings; let us not live, work, and die without furthering the cause of the entire race. Indeed, life is choices; let us choose to unite our families and our nations into One Body, choose to nourish our beings with the light of One Vision, choose to coexist in peace and harmony under One Kingdom. There is no direction for us to head except forward, towards The Light, nowhere for us to journey to but home, to the glorious kingdom that awaits us. The vessels of a great life story are progress and growth; let us progress and grow until we can do so no more and make the story of the human race one of ultimate triumph. Let us bring forth and breathe life into The Global Utopian Kingdom!!

THE END

Addendum:

One Man, One Vision, One Kingdom

1.1I sleep not, nor am I awake; consciousness I have transcended, with a third eye, I see. 1.2Here and now I exist, never do I cease to dream, light and color I respire.. 1.3Aware I am of that which is present and that which is missing, this reality I have recognized as a rendition, solemnly I have beared witness to the prescribing of the mission. 1.4That which is hidden has been unveiled to me, that which is manifest has laid bare The Great Truths before me, of a mighty and glorious kingdom, I have visions..

2.1These visions of a global utopian kingdom emanate from the wellspring of The Great Within.. 2.2The Endless Reservoir which flows into my being suffices to cleanse all earth, to purify all life; anew shall be the world, fresh shall be the morning.. 2.3A new era shall dawn, a new beginning shall unfold, the living shall once again be whole..

3.1The earth in its entirety shall be a wellspring of infinite goodness, the blessings of Liberty, Justice, Peace, and Prosperity nourishing all.. 3.2This is the tomorrow that belongs to man, this is what awaits him if strong and wise. 3.3Yet, howbeit that what is before him has hitherto eluded him?? 3.4Lo! Man's promised glory will only be brought forth by his growth; he shall be exalted only once ready, worthy..

4.1Growth alters form and essence.. Growth brings into existence that which was once naught.. 4.2At present, The Kingdom is but a seed within man. 4.3It shall attain maturity only as he does, blossom into fullness only as he does.. 4.4As man transforms himself, so too shall he transform the world around him. 4.5The tools he requires lie within him; with strength and wisdom can he carve out a tomorrow ideal.

5.1In its present state, the world is The Great Uncarved Block..

5.2The eyes which make contact with the outer world cannot see that which light hits not, but the heart which is whole may perceive form which is yet to manifest amidst the formless.. 5.3The man and woman well-cultivated receive well visions of The Kingdom, with sure vision do such behold the promise of tomorrow.

6.1Well-cultivated men and women are the soil in which The Kingdom takes root.. 6.2Such men and women give life to The Kingdom, such provide light for tomorrow.. 6.3Behold! Magnificent is The Kingdom, and even more magnificent are the Men and Women of The Kingdom!

7.1Graceful, dignified, goodly, are The Men and Women of The Kingdom.. 7.2They hold life dear, they harm not the cause of the living; one they are with nature.. 7.3Sentient beings have their mercy, modest are they in sacrificing lower creatures. 7.4Unto one another they are kind, unto to one another they are helpful. 7.5Unto to one another do they smile and offer warmth; most beautiful are they.. 7.6Their beauty emanates from within, radiating from the goodness in their core; forever they are young, forever are they vigorous. 7.7Humbly do they walk, humbly do they speak. 7.8Illness touches them not, for they are pure in heart, worthy.. precious, they are. 7.9Great care they take in dealing with one another, in inhabiting the earth.. Their existence is purified, nourishing.. 7.10That which is difficult is made easy for them, trouble they overcome. 7.11Lo! Hardship is a weakly foe before them, the strength of one supporting all.. 7.12These are the last to walk the earth, their descent heralding The End of Times..

8.1Much work is to be done to prepare the earth for The Men and Women of The Kingdom, much is to be done to elevate man and the conditions of life. 8.2The Great Work is but the only true work for Mankind.. It must commence at once. 8.3Let a man lead if he know the way, let mankind follow if goodness is known. 8.4Let the day be long for The People, let time be precious to them. 8.5Let men, women, and children know their role, let them delight to honor duty. 8.6Let the wise direct the strong, let the strong care for weak. 8.7Let fear not overcome The People.. Bravery is indispensable to the cause. 8.8Let those who hear come forth and witness what is at stake. 8.9Let enemies see the light in unity. 8.10In unity, let friends march forth to defeat greed. 8.11Let every man partake in the bounty of the earth, let every a one be seen and heard. 8.12Let none be denied dignity, everywhere and forever.

9.1Goodness is everlasting, good is the carrying out of The Great Work. 9.2Good is contribution to the cause of The Kingdom, good is humility.. 9.3Good is selflessness, good is sacrifice. 9.4Good are the men and women who work for one another, good are the silent and still.. 9.5All who sacrifice for The Kingdom shall triumph, all who resist The Kingdom shall fail.. 9.6None exercising free will shall be exempt from duty.. 9.7All who love shall find peace.. 9.8Relief shall find those who fight, torment awaits the traitors of humanity. 9.9In vanity do the enemies of The Kingdom scheme against tomorrow, for lo! Tomorrow schemes against them! 9.10It was written, but who can testify to this other than he with the pen?? 9.11Good, are the words which begin and end.. 9.12Mercy.. straight not is the line connecting the twain..

10.1The will of man was set free, so his path became obscure.. 10.2Verily, the last chapters of his story shall tell of ignominy and doom, glory and triumph.. 10.3Behold! There are countless paths he may take, yet he will meet but with one fate! 10.4And lo! Man has created innumerable divisions amongst himself and segmented his brothers and sisters into numerous states.

10.5Yet alas, unity among infinite division is the way of the universe, so then let one man embody and reflect the goodness of all humanity, let one vision illuminate the hearts of all who believe in tomorrow, let the promise of one kingdom fill every corner of the earth with light and hope!

11.1Tomorrow is bright. Today is dim. 11.2To today belongs savages, to tomorrow, men. 11.3Against the current must men deliver on the promise of tomorrow, against the tides of hatred, greed, and selfishness shall glory and triumph flow.. 11.4Early does arrive the instinct of men to lie, compete, work mischief. 11.5Late does arrive the ability of men to stand upright, cooperate, work wonders.. 11.6It is like the savage to watch his brother starve. 11.7It is like the savage to make war. 11.8It is like him to choose unworthy fights.. 11.9It is like the man upright to take from his plate to feed his brother. 11.10It is like the man upright to make peace. 11.11It is like him to fight for Liberty and Justice. 11.12None are so strong as the man upright, as he stands the savages shall fall.. 11.13As he stands to face the world the sun shall rise to face Him. 11.14As the sun rises to greet him, the day of the savage shall come to a close, The Kingdom shall be alive.

12.1The air of The Kingdom shall be sweet, refreshing; The Man Upright abides not filth and pollution.. 12.2His food shall be wholesome, nutritious. 12.3His water pure, unsullied.. 12.4He takes care to farm food correctly; he is patient, gentle.. 12.5Great care does He take to manage his farm, great care does He take to manage his family. 12.6He abides not illness and discord, health and concord being vital to his peace. 12.7He prospers for the earth is bountiful and his brother modest, generous.. 12.8He lacks no good thing, his life is fulfilling..

13.1The uncontrolled desires of the savage and his foolishness has caused men to bleed, starve, sorrow. 13.2Lo! The Heedless Savage shall be exiled from the kingdom if not crushed by The Man Upright! 13.3Lo! He has no place among virtuous men and women, no right to influence children! 13.4His infidelity shall not taint The Kingdom, his era has passed.. 13.5His utility lies in illuminating the path not be taken..

14.1The straight path shall be illuminated by The Man Upright, he will lead the way to a tomorrow bright, full of promise. 14.2The words he speaks are true, his actions sincere.. 14.3His steps are purposeful and his purpose is The Kingdom. 14.4Progress and growth is the purpose of man, The Kingdom represents the culmination of his progress and growth. 14.5It is that which he shall receive when polished, when worthy.. 14.6It is the ripened fruit of millennia of toil and struggle. 14.7It is the crowning of man fully formed and mature. 14.8It is the destiny of Man once strong and wise; his final resting place, his final abode.

15.1His home current is hostile, unclean.. 15.2Life is uncomfortable, Life is under threat.. 15.3Weapons of war abound, wildlife is under pressure. 15.4The earth is sick, the wholesome has mixed with the toxic. 15.5Changes uncontrolled, in rapid succession, sweep the planet. 15.6Men foolish and weak and selfish lead The People, stunting their growth, stymying their maturation. 15.7Competing nations are filled with men mislead, righteous and unrighteous indignation. 15.8Hope and Shame are at risk of being lost -of this mankind cannot bear the cost. 15.9Children are blinded, those of age rendered deaf; numbness lurks about.. 15.10Depression and dismay have invaded countless homes, Fear and anxiety penetrate every corner of the Earth. 15.11Enemies hide in plain sight, friends are unorganized, unready to fight.. ^{15.12}Unbeknownst to the masses, The Great War is but underway..

^{16.1}The Enemies of The Kingdom have arrayed themselves against The Kingdom, and lo! They have arrayed themselves against Mankind! ^{16.2}They seek to undermine the will, the power of the masses; they are powerful, cunning.. ^{16.3}They fear greatest a king just and virtuous; a champion of the people, a relentless defender.. ^{16.4}The subjection of the masses to their will is what they seek, to have free reign over the earth, to be sovereigns.. ^{16.5}And lo! They have hoarded wealth and the bounty of the earth, schemed in government, commandeered states and industries! ^{16.6}A people unaware do but lie at their mercy..

^{17.1}Every move plotted by the enemy is strategic, tactical, devised to divide the people, devised to delay the tomorrow awaited by the good and noble. ^{17.2}Every move plotted by the enemy must be countered by the masses united, resolute. ^{17.3}Men and women wise and strong must emerge to lead the people, to ensure victory in battle.. ^{17.4}Great Tests are life, and to those who endure, The Battle Tested, belong tomorrow..

^{18.1}Magnificent springs of hope and joy await The Destined Victors of the great war, they shall live in peace, end their lives in peace. ^{18.2}They shall prosper all their days, their progeny all their days. ^{18.3}They shall soar afloat the winds of liberty, dwell in the comfort of justice. ^{18.4}Their king shall preside over their kingdom, they shall preside over their king. ^{18.5}Every man's place within the kingdom shall be secure, the role of every man made clear. ^{18.6}Duty shall be honored, the honorable held dear. ^{18.7}The Kingdom being global, nowhere shall an external enemy appear. ^{18.8}The internal worlds of The Men and Women

of The Kingdom at peace, The Enemies of The Kingdom vanquished, there shall be no reason to fear..

19.1There shall come a time when Time itself shall be still, everything will be alive, but there will be nothing to kill.. 19.2Nothing shall be beyond grasp, there shall be nothing to await.. 19.3No records shall be kept, there will be no need for dates. 19.4The present shall be, men shall be, all that is shall simply, be. 19.5None shall be exposed, nor shall any hide. 19.6Goodness will abound, humility shall overcome pride. 19.7There shall be forgiveness for he who once lied, there shall be a home for he who forsook humanity. 19.8There shall be nothing to sell, nor stories to tell, no wickedness to fell, there shall be life to live..

20.1Precious are the honest, precious are the pure. 20.2Precious is the timeless, precious is its lure.. 20.3Precious are those who love deeply, precious are those who smile sincerely. 20.4Precious are those who dream clearly, precious are those who nurture the seedling.. 20.5Precious is the man who envisions for the sake of humanity, precious is the vision which uplifts and guides humanity, precious is the kingdom which completes humanity..

Hear Ye, Hear Ye: Alas, Thus He Speaketh His Peace:

Here, are we now, towards The Kingdom, we are going.. The time, the place, the people, have all been chosen. Be strong, O people, and take care to endure. Weakness is ever costly, regrettable is forfeiture.. Indefensible is the forsaking of duty, reprehensible is the failure to live truly.. Verily, life is hard -this has always been well known. Be ye heedful and come back home, prepare thyselves for glory! The Kingdom has been ordained for thee, as has peace and prosperity. Love and let thy heart be thy guide, set men free and treat each other justly. Blessed and sacred are those who sacrifice and serve mankind nobly, and behold! Exalted shall be those who live, speak, and walk humbly..

Know thy place, and delight therein. Be vigilant in warding off evil, in abstaining from sin. What is coming cannot be prevented, from a time before was it ordained.. Save disbelief, naught is there to be lamented, for disbelievers, naught is there to be obtained. Believe ye in The Kingdom! A promise true and unfailing.. The Earth was created for Man, what is therein, for his taming.

Work! and delight in the fruits thereof! Grow! and delight in the yields thereof! Conquer thyselves, thy triumph shall be indeed everlasting.. Emerge from thy trials victorious, fully formed, a tree from a sapling. Reach for thy destiny, know that it lies not beyond thy grasp. Verily, all shall be given to him who believeth and asks..